**Wendy Lee Hermance**

# where i'm going with this poem

*Selected Poems*

Translation: José Lima

Formatting: Rachel Bostwick

"Wendy Lee Hermance's prose and poetry are made of touching and surprising childhood memories – of shriveled apples, old pillows, fallen tree limbs, imaginary radio stations and things so difficult to put into words that we can only glimpse them between the lines of this highly compelling work."

Richard Zimler, author,
*The Gospel According to Lazarus*

The prose and poetry in Wendy Lee Hernance's personal narrative comprise a unique memoir beginning with richly detailed childhood experiences, moving through adolescence, ultimately manifesting in adulthood. *Where I'm Going with this Poem*, is a hymn to "this lovely human mess" that is the speaker's life, but this is a life filled with a myriad of experiences, all described with a poet's empathy and attention to detail reminding us all, as Hernance did in the last poem of the collection, of our capacity to *find some things to love*.

Marjory Wentworth,
*South Carolina Poet Laureate*

*In memory of my mother, Nancy Lee Hermance. For journalists, soldiers, activists, children, and for anyone who tells the truth, yet is not believed.*

*My grandmother, Dot, and her brother, Roland.*

# CONTENTS

# When I was Little
## 2019

My first memories were of living with my father, my mother and my brother in Florham Park, New Jersey in a tiny, 18th century frame house on an endless, bare back yard that sloped into a woods. The land must have been farmed at one time, though the soil was dry and sandy. We had a rusty, used slide that ended in a small sand pile, and that was it.

Inside, the house was never finished. My father tore the walls out and we lived with open cavities. This was interesting for what he found and showed me; a tiny bisque doll known as a *Frozen Charlotte*, and a black, shriveled, leather shoe of a little child. Outside, my second-story bedroom window faced a busy road, but was well-protected by a huge and fragrant lilac tree. To this day I love flowers and the color lilac is especially mine.

Across the street lived a Japanese family in a modern split-level house. My mother would visit their mother for tea, bringing us along. I think they had a well-behaved boy and girl a few years older than us, who paid us no attention. Their mother gave us *travelling plums*; salty, sweet and licorice-flavored. Some were dry and hard and needed to be sucked and nibbled at before the thin fruit separated from the seed. Others were soft and gooey, like the insides of soft dates. They were wrapped in double wrappers, signifying their specialness.

Otherwise I ate carrots, so many carrots! I was never without one clutched in my fist at this time, so that one visitor - a nasty and presumptuous man, who might have been a Realtor appraising our house for foreclosure because we lost it soon after - told me I would get "carrot poisoning" and my skin would turn orange. Even at the age of four, I knew the man was an idiot. He was pasty-skinned and smoking a cigarette as he criticized my diet. He knew nothing of value.

We also had a dog named Percival, or Percy. He was a *Wire-Haired Terrier* from the pound. The otherwise perfectly-tailored little chap had been hurt and his jaw was crooked so he appeared to be smiling all the time. He loved us so that he let us push and drag him up the steep, metal slide steps and push him down the polished steel chute. At the bottom he waited patiently allowing us to cover him in sand, wincing but without complaint. Allegedly he bit the mail man. Allegedly he made my brother allergic. When we moved into my grandmother's house, he was disappeared. This was my first brush with injustice.

From Florham Park we had moved to Madison, the next town over, into the half-timbered Tudor my grandfather had built. My grandfather had just died by then. His name was James Alexander Smith, although this was a made-up name as he was a foundling. He was a bit aloof, (although also sick). He was a circuit court judge and a successful insurance and real estate man, who probably never had much time for children. I remember Sunday lunches with my grandfather, the drive to Howard Johnsons restaurant for fried clam strips and chocolate-chip-mint ice cream, dyed an elegant, bluish-green pastel. This was a very fancy occasion for us. I would be dressed in a party dress with wide crinoline, and a ribbon sash tied in a bow at my back. To this day I will never pass up fried clams with tomato ketchup. I have painted the walls to every home I have lived in for 25 years in a similar ice cream pale green.

Soon after we moved into her house my grandmother moved out. She moved to the next town over, Chatham, into a brand-new apartment complex. In her Spartan way, it was a one-bedroom. She outfitted the room with twin beds painted white, except for small oval decals of 18th Century French pic nickers. It had one bath room, tiled walls and floor in the pink of a happy cartoon pig. This may have been a sign of her ironic sense of humor. Everything else about her was understated. My grandmother always had a stylish car. I remember her elegant, black bodied, white-topped Studebaker Hawk parked beneath the beech tree in our leaf-littered, macadam driveway. Her next car was a white VW with red vinyl interior. It was probably a Type 3, Notchback hatchback. This would have been around 1963.

I was always impressed with my grandmother's car savvy and proud to drive with her in her car. She otherwise spent next to nothing on herself, wearing the same, charcoal-grey wool pencil skirt and white, lace adorned, short-sleeved blouse every day in three seasons. In the summer she rotated three cheap, sleeveless, nylon shift dresses in abstract prints. They were bought from Robert Hall and cost $6 each. The one I remember her wearing most was also black and white. In all weather she wore a full girdle that included the bra, and sheer hose. I never recall her getting cold. She moved with a bustling march and she whisper-whistled little ditties she made up as she went about her business. I have never owned a nylon shift, but I remember pausing in 2012 mid slice above a block of sharp cheddar cheese in my Sydney kitchen, because I realized that I was wearing a charcoal grey pencil skirt and a frilly white, short-sleeved blouse, preparing the same crumbly, velvety cheese I´d watched her prepare for me countless times wearing the same outfit.

Her married name was Dorothy DeWarren Smith. Her father was a Waller and my name was once pointed out to me in the pages of *Debretts Peerage and Baronetage*. My mother´s first cousin, Bobby lived a world away from us - in Massachusetts. He had inherited the title *Baronet* along with a small castle. I met him only twice and briefly at our house.

My grandmother was a proper Victorian lady, who had once been a fun-loving girl. She taught us games like *Come She Comes*, a version of *I Spy*, and *Ghost*, a spelling game well-played in a car. She was now saddled with some responsibility for her daughter´s wrong choices. She smoked occasional Tareytown cigarettes, the kind advertised with people with a black eye captioned *I´d rather fight than switch*, until she switched to Parliaments. We called her *Little Gram*, and knew that she had been called "Dot" by her friends as a girl. She had no local friends, but once her childhood friend, Mignon came to visit. I remember walking into my grandmother´s apartment bedroom to see a plump, completely naked woman seated on my grandmother´s dressing stool brushing her long, chestnut brown hair, which fell below her hips. She must have been in her 60s. She turned to me without getting up or covering up to chat with me pleasantly. That was Mignon.

On Sundays my family went to *Little Gram´s* for lavish meals she made us; top quality roasts of meat with small round, roasted potatoes, side dishes of artichokes, and always a beautiful green salad with ripe, red tomatoes and avocado slices. This was at a time when salads were being concocted of Jello and mini marshmallows. She also served only whole wheat *Hollywood* brand bread and used *Hollywood* brand safflower oil. I have no idea where she found such things back then. We ate off *Mayflower Vernon Kilns California Pottery* that she may have bought on a long-distant visit to her wild, younger sister, Miram, who lived in Los Gatos.

My father´s car was *the Old Merc*. It was a massive tank of polished rust that he loved. Its interior was heavy wool in a beige and rust-brown stripe like blankets. It was in perfect shape. We slept in the back seat, but I remember most standing next to my father as he drove, leaning against his shoulder. This is how tall the cabin was. He would tune the radio to the classical music station or to big-band jazz with lush instrumentals and he would discuss the music with us. My mother´s car was a green station wagon, always for work, always a mess. She did not enjoy driving and I hated being in that car and was not in it often.

My father dropped out of school in the 4th grade to work during the Great Depression. He cleaned up construction sites. He met my mother when they were both volunteers at a community theatre, she a budding actress and he a carpenter building sets. My father told me how he bought a box of *Nabisco Ginger Snaps* and ate them for his lunch with a quart of milk. The other food he told me about was buckwheat pancakes -which were somehow available to buy back then in normal grocery stores as a mix.  My father brought me salted pretzel sticks from the bar he favored, *Flynn´s Tavern*. I always called them *prenzils*. I went to *Flynn´s Tavern* with him a few times. The other working-class men were always kind to me. The pretzels came in small, flat, white cardboard boxes that served as elegant serving trays once the clear cellophane top had been peeled off. They were *Ballantine* brand to go with the *Ballantine* beer. We picked at the *prenzils* daintily as if they were a great delicacy, licking our fingers to collect the course salt crystals in the corners of the box, (although sometimes we grabbed fists of them and shoved them in our mouths). My father also brought home apples for us, a single apple. With the few beers and the pretzels they were all he could afford from the allowance my mother gave him. My parents fought all the time, possibly about money, and probably also about the unbreachable divide of *class*.

What my father could not give in material things, he made up for by sharing his time and his imagination. The other fathers were all successful executives working in New York City, or at Bell Labs or Sandoz, or one of the other nearby New Jersey pharmaceutical or chemical companies. Their corporate headquarters were always set on vast, green lawns. At least some of the other men may have had a grudging respect for my father for the time that he spent with their kids.

## The Circle
In the winter, my father tied together the neighborhood kids´ two-

blade sleds, one to each other like train cars, and he pulled us around *The Circle*, the big, round park that fronted our houses. For this he used my mother´s station wagon with the tailgate open. Whenever one of us got too cold or, rarely, fell off the slow-moving train, a call was raised, my father would stop the car and the child would climb into the back of the wagon to ride in the car the rest of the time. He always carried a thermos or a pot of hot chocolate in the back to warm us. One year I had a Flying Saucer, a new, red rubber disc with grooves like a concave vinyl record. It was something novel, but it spun over the ice uncontrollably, throwing off our orderly formation and making me nervous and dizzy. I think it was understood that this was an experiment and it was alright to fail.

Around Christmas every year there was a neighborhood bonfire in *The Circle* for *caroling*. My father seemed to be in charge of the fire. For days or a week or more in advance, men would deposit firewood in the pile, which we saw growing outside across from our homes. There were plenty of trees in the neighborhood to gather fallen limbs from. No one bought wood. Even though it was an upscale neighborhood, no one fussed over *a lawn* or had a yard service like people of any status seem to feel obligated to have now. Spending time with family was then valued in the US. Even well-paid workers were secure enough to keep to a 40-hour work week, leaving time to do their own yards with their kids.

My father and maybe one or two of the other men would light the fire and we would slowly trickle out on the *caroling* evening. We sang around the fire to warm up before breaking off into a roving choir to serenade the elderly and any neighbors who happened to be home sick that year. There was usually a good crowd of maybe 20 or thirty neighbors. It was always cold. Usually there would be snow and it might be raining. We went anyway. At the end we convened in the house of one neighbor for hot chocolate and cookies, or had the treats outside back at the fire if no one had volunteered to host a bunch of muddy galoshes that year. The event gave me a sense of community and egalitarianism and also, of continuity. Even though our house was falling down, I was skinny and unkempt, with matted hair and wore used clothes and my mother illegally sold antiques from the house, we were woven into the fabric of this community. This may have been out of deference to my late grandfather´s legacy, although I prefer to believe it was out of an inherent New Jersey kindness and recognition of value above price.

In nice weather we played kickball in *The Circle*. It was easy to have friends. You just looked outside to see who was about or you went and knocked on a few doors until you found someone home and a snack. In the summers at dusk my father would head out to *The Circle* with one of his thin, white handkerchiefs with a few small pebbles tied inside to weight it. Kids gradually came out of their houses after dinner to join us as he threw the handkerchiefs up into the air, attracting dark silhouettes of shrieking bats. They swooped down to grab the handkerchiefs, sometimes catching in our hair. This caused us to shriek, too.

*The Fog Man,* also brought us outside to play together. This was a truck that drove around *The Circle* spraying insecticide. We ran after the truck dancing and laughing open-mouthed in the thick, trailing fog calling the others to join us. *The Fog* had an oily, sweet taste. In 1962 Rachel Carson's book, *Silent Spring* came out, initiating regulation — only - of DDT. DDT was made at Ciga-Geigy two towns over in Summit, New Jersey. We began calling out to each other, *The Fog Man! The Fog Man!* as soon as we spotted the truck, in the same way we sounded the alarm for *The Ice Cream Man! The Ice Cream Man!* When the *Ice Cream Man* appeared, we were desperate to get our hands on some money before the truck left and we missed our chance, which always felt like a once-in-a-lifetime opportunity. I stuck with the *Sky Blue Pop* because it was the cheapest option and I could usually convince my mother and because it was a beautiful shade of blue that tasted of fake raspberries. Once or twice I had extra money to try the *Royale Sundae,* which cost twice the price of the straight-forward pop of water, sugar and synthetic color and flavoring. Really, I did not care for the mushy, frozen chocolate wafer crumbs and calling these ingredients smashed together in a sugar cone, a *sundae* seemed just pretentious. Briefly I tried switching to *Dreamsicles,* a new thing also allegedly more sophisticated than ice pops, but I was never convinced that the orange-flavored ice pop outside with vanilla ice cream in was a good flavor or a good texture combination. Rarely had I the extra 15 cents, anyway. Also, I preferred showing off the more unusual blue lips and tongue that the *Sky Blue Pop* left, to the red and orange dyed mouths more common in the neighborhood. It was a bargain all the way around.

# Neighbors

I spent a lot of time directly across *The Circle* from my house at the Ryans´ house. From the age of five I began developing more of a Midwestern accent than a New Jersey accent due to my time with the Ryan family. They had moved from Iowa because Mr. Ryan, *Robert*, joined First National Bank in New York as a Vice President. I remember him as a genuinely kind man, working at home from the dining room table, stopping to show interest in me and his children. My friend was Mary Beth, the oldest of the four Ryan kids. Below her was Rob, then Joe, the only blond member of the family. Joe had an explosive emotional character and we called him *Little Joe* after the charismatic, youngest son on TV´s *Bonanza*. Finally, there was baby Kate. Except for Joe, the Ryans all had straight brown hair and light brown eyes, like their dad.

Mrs. Ryan, *Marge*, had blue eyes. She was an avid reader and researcher of everything, often in support of her children`s interests, and even any I could articulate. She could often be seen marching past our house on the path that led from *The Circle* into Drew University, carrying a large satchel of books to and from the university library. Mrs. Ryan was a worrier and a problem solver and she was so forthright that I recall her telling us that her doctor told her to wear a bra to bed at night to keep her breasts from sagging. I don't know if she had just come in from the doctor that day and spoke out in frustration, or if we were in a discussion about our own growing, or not-growing breasts at the moment, but the Ryans´ refreshing earthiness and lack of pretension set them far above anyone else I knew in New Jersey. I couldn´t get enough of them.

Mary Beth and I spent our time in the sunroom or the kitchen, or the living room of their house. They did not entertain friends in the bedrooms. In the sunroom we made up songs and our own notation system to keep track of them on an old, upright piano painted mint green. Our system was to write numbers directly onto the ivory piano keys, using different colors of wax crayon. The keys stayed marked in purple 3s, and 4s, yellow 4's, and green 6s, each color given an order so that purple might be the first note struck the number of times notated, then the yellow note would be struck its notated number of times, and so on. The system was obviously flawed. It depended on shared memory and discussion. We tried to notate it in a notebook, and we named each song, but someone ran off with the notebook for another purpose. We never worked out the kinks and we never got in trouble for marking the keys and our system was never erased.

We also gathered in the sunroom to watch *The Three Stooges* on a small, black and white television set. I was never as keen watching people smashing each other over the head as Mary Beth was. A serious child who devoured books and later studied physics at Cornell, she explained she needed it to *wash over her brains*, when I questioned the show´s appeal. Her mother expressed similar concern over the violence, but always gave us wide margins to do our own exploring.

We were often in their kitchen cooking experimentally, or crammed in their dark breakfast nook as her mother cooked from *Gourmet* magazine or *Mastering the Art of French Cooking*. She would tut-tut like a hen over things not turning out as in the pictures. We, meanwhile experimented with cakes of ground acorns "like the Indians." Probably we had instructions courtesy of Drew library or the little public library down Green Village Road with its glass floor scuffed translucent like beach glass. Our cakes were a bitter disappointment. Maybe our acorns were collected in the wrong season, or we skipped out on the laborious parboiling and drying procedures needed to turn squirrel food edible.

Our apple pies were more successful. We often stole apples from the gigantic apple tree in the Holden´s back yard, three doors down from Mary Beth´s house. It was next to the Schwartzes, a childless couple with two cinnamon-colored dachshunds. The Holden´s house was wooden and painted red like a barn. The Holden´s were older with grown kids and I am sure they delighted in watching us secretly from their window as we stole their apples. Mrs. Holden ruined our fun forever when she left the house one day, bringing us a bag to fill. As much as we liked our apple pies, they never were as delicious as when we stole the apples to make them.

The Holden´s apple tree was OK to climb, but it was filled with poking suckers, so when we wanted to climb a tree, we usually went down the path alongside my house into Drew University. We passed the new, orange brick student center, passed the 19th century granite library, and went all the way to the back of the campus behind the *Grace B Linden Garden* to *the apartment tree*. It was a heroically large beech tree at the center of an abandoned orchard. It was so enormous that it could hold six kids at once, each separated in his own *apartment*. We rarely beat the birds to the few cherries and hard pears that managed to develop, so the main attraction to the orchard was the climbing tree.

We thought nothing of the mile or mile and a half walk through campus to get to it.

The *Grace B Linden Garden* was a special spot where Mary Beth and I played *Indians*. No one else ever joined us in this game and no one else seemed to know about the place at all. It had a simple pipe trickling water down from a small rise over some rocks. At one side of the man-made spring was a quarter of a submerged mill stone. At the top of the rise a long hedge row backed two low, horizontal cedar trees that met, forming a neat little cave perfect for two crouching children. There was a faded, red barn 30 feet behind our cave that no one ever visited. We would carry forsythia "whips" from the path along my house on the way and strip their bark, calling it *snake skin*. The spongey, inner core - looking like wood filler - we called *Indian chewing gum*. It wasn´t bad. It had a mild, green taste. We hauled dried mud chips from flat-bottomed gullies that had been wet then dried and cracked, leaving the heavier sand and stones below and just the fine mud risen, in paint cans we collected at the new subdivision construction site about two miles away. Using the pipe water, we reconstituted the chips at our spot, forming *Indian pottery*. We left our pots along with our *snakeskins* to dry on the exposed mill stone. We came back days or weeks later and all would be untouched, although the pots often crumbled in our hands.

A lot of our time was spent sneaking around. When not sneaking around the subdivision construction site, or screaming as loudly as we could in the Drew University woods – a professional technique for clearing the throat to prepare the voice to sing, according to Mary Beth - or stealing apples, we were sneaking around the university science building. We passed the familiar dark oak and wavy glass cases full of glass specimen jars containing faded, pickled embryos, brains, hearts and ears, whispering and running to hide whenever we heard echoing footsteps. No one ever bothered us or told us to leave. I don´t recall ever seeing anyone, except maybe a janitor, though I recall we were very good at hiding.

Sometimes on our rounds we passed through a conference room with a large, polished wood table in the center, surrounded by oil paintings of former college presidents. The paintings were a bit creepy and looked down on us disapprovingly from the walls. But then, we didn´t care. We were alive and young. They weren´t.

The first time I saw marijuana was around the same time David Kirkpatrick stuck his hands down my pants and put his fingers inside me. I must have been nine. It happened very quickly. He was a grotesque, blubbery guy with weak eyes. His little sister, Kathy and I were friends, though I never enjoyed being at their house. It was deathly quiet except for a loudly ticking grandfather clock inside their front door. They had thick, new Oriental rugs. Their house would be considered *curated* today. They had, for example, a Swedish Modern leather office chair when everyone else at the time made do with old, scuffed oak chairs with their carved-out bottom shape on the seats. We were sitting on the couch in their sunroom that day, watching television and I wriggled away immediately not because I felt violated, but because I was embarrassed and felt the need to explain that I wasn´t wearing underpants that day because they were all in the wash. That was undoubtedly true, but the pants were soft, worn, loose denim jeans lined in cotton flannel and I would have worn them without underpants, anyway.

The first time I saw marijuana it couldn´t have been later than 1964. It was two doors down the other direction from my house in the home of Jeanne Shockley. Mrs. Shockley was the ex-wife of William Shockley, known then as "the inventor of the transistor." (He wasn´t really that and later he was shunned as a proponent of eugenics. But, he truly was the founder of Silicon Valley after he left his wife, Jeanne and moved to Mountain View, California and began a semi-conductor company there.) It was with either their son, Richard or their son, William who was visiting his mother at the time. He called me into his room to show me his bed covered with the small, dried leaves. There were many pounds of them.

This has got to be a testament to bad parenting. Not so much that he was selling drugs – that was quite enterprising at the time as he seemed to have gotten in on ground floor of the market – but because a grown man sought to impress an ignorant, little nine-year old. The meaning of what I was looking at was entirely lost on me, of course. I shrugged and walked out and did realize or remember what I had seen for many years after. The young man had long brown hair approaching his waist, which was also very unusual for the East Coast at this time. Probably he was also living in California.

That was the only time I remember seeing one of the Shockley kids, though I spent a lot of time visiting their mother. Mrs. Shockley would find little jobs for me, washing a few dishes, chopping vegetables or helping her bake with white flour and sugar. She was a dumpling-looking woman with charcoal grey hair, like a like a soft-bodied, *apple head doll*. The most distinguishing thing I remember about her was her thick, off-white wool bobby socks worn with comfortable lace-up shoes and a dress or skirt and blouse and a long, cardigan sweater worn all year round. Around their house they had large, crystal things mainly amber in color, the size of several grownup fists put together. Mrs. Shockley said they were the result of failed laboratory experiments of her ex-husband.

The Shockley house was dark brick next to an empty lot with a few scraggly apple trees, too little to bother climbing.  It was one of the older houses on the street. Like mine, it was built in the 1920s and maybe 1800 square feet in size, with charming little details like round windows and window seats, a second story sunroom and an arched front door. All our houses on the street featured sunrooms. Probably for my whole life I have been looking for a house like this one.

Most of the fathers on the street, with the exception of Mr. Ryan, seemed to be stressed out. Even as a little kid I could probably have told you who was screwing around, drinking heavily, maybe even abusing their wives or kids. I'm sure Jean Kirkpatrick, the most-soft spoken and absent person I have ever met, was heavily medicated. Mrs. O´Donnell was frequently drunk, as she was when she ordered me to remove the chewing gum she blamed me for getting stuck in her daughter, Chrissie´s hair. This was something that I had little or nothing to do with. I liked Chrissie. I felt sorry for her. She was bullied by her older brothers.  A Ukrainian family moved next to the Ryan´s house for a time. That little boy was the saddest, most stressed-out child I ever met. He looked exactly like Charlie Brown with his large, round head and sparse hair and his misery. I wish I could remember his name. He was such a sweet kid.

The houses on our street were all wonderful, two stories, plus attics and basements. Most were built between the 1920s and thirties, though a few may have been a little older. In our tribal snobbery, we considered the smaller, older houses the best and quietly pitied those who lived in the newer houses. The kids in the new subdivision being built next to ours we would barely associate with. We considered those houses substandard, and their owners the crass nouveau riche, though we did not know that term at the time. As frequent visitors to the houses under construction to collect our mud chips and to cut out the colored telephone wires we all collected and traded amongst ourselves, we had some actual expertise in this matter. As we easily pried open basement windows and doors in our search for exotic, yellow and brown spotted *giraffe wire*, or neon lime and dark teal *lizard* wire for our shoebox collections, we were learning something about residential construction. Two decades later I began a career restoring old houses and have never quite stopped.

Though we liked the popular Perelli kids, we pitied them their new split-level house. We were rarely invited inside. Mr. Perelli I barely recall seeing, but his father lived with them and would sit out in the driveway and keep an eye on the street, whittling or cracking walnuts, always doing something with his hands. I am not sure that he spoke English. There were four Perelli boys, *the Twins,* Thomas and Stephen, and their older brothers David and Charles. Their mom had dark hair pulled back and glasses and very dark, almost black eyes. She always seemed worried, but in the good way that you would want a mom to worry about four, wild boys. All seemed like happy, normal kids, each with his own interests and personality, something I count as a proof of coming from a happy home.

We also had a retarded kid named Artie who was never seen without the string he sucked on, pulling it up and down into his mouth as one would work a yo-yo. His lips were always bright red. It may have started as a red string, or maybe he was drinking red Kool-Aid, or on a medication dyed red, like a cherry- flavored cough syrup. Maybe his lips were just always irritated. Artie spoke only in modulated two-syllable grunts, which was a little creepy, but otherwise, he seemed to be okey and he fit in with the rest of us.

One day the Ryans came home from a vacation. The family were downstairs after putting baby Kate to bed upstairs, when they heard a blood-curdling scream. They ran upstairs to find Artie peering over the crib at baby Kate. Somehow, he had let himself into their house while they were away. In characteristic fashion, the Ryans did not seem to think he had meant any harm, and made little of the incident.

After Mrs. Shockley passed away or moved away – no one except Mrs. Ryan ever told me anything, and she never mentioned this transition – the Witte family moved in. Mr. Witte worked for the Polish Embassy. I was only twelve when I began babysitting for George, Douglas and baby Susan. George was only a few years younger than I was. It meant a lot to me to be trusted by their parents, though I think Mr. Witte had his doubts. In truth, the kids were pretty rambunctious and strong-willed. Possibly no one else would sit them at all and certainly not at my beginner's rate. I devised a *magic trick* to keep them in line. If they agreed to brush their teeth and go straight to bed, I would perform my *magic trick*. Once in their pajamas, scrubbed and ready for bed, they would gather around a simple glass of water in their kitchen. I then placed a cloth over the glass and said a few magic words. When I pulled off the cloth the water had transformed into root beer, orange, grape or lemon-lime soda pop. I had lucked into a vast supply of *Fizzies* from a school friend whose dad worked at Warner-Lambert. As luck would have it, my luck was concurrent with the product's recall because its artificial sweetener, cyclamate, had been found to cause cancer. I did not know this until now.

I began writing poems about this time. I found an old fountain pen in a sewing chest that my mother had gotten at an estate sale, complete with its contents of wooden spools of dry-rotted silk thread, thimbles, needle threaders and an assortment of ancient pens and graphite pencil stubs. Since I had no ink to go in the pen and no way to get any, I used food coloring found in the back of a one of the metal kitchen cabinets, left from long-ago Easter egg dying. Green was the color I chose. I worked the tiny lever on the side of the pen shaft to siphon up the dye. It worked perfectly! I do not recall ever having notebook paper or art supplies of any kind in the house, nor books or magazines, but I tore pieces of brown paper from grocery sacks to write on. This worked out just fine and lent a bohemian appeal. I filled a *Brown Betty* teapot with *Constant Comment* tea liberally sugared and sat late into the evening at the dirty, round oak pedestal table, writing slowly with the ornate, engraved pen nib.  I don't have any of those scraps of paper, but here is part of one poem that I remember writing then:

*With what arrogance I cast*
*small poems like pearls on the sea*
*and expect them to float.*


In my preteens and teens there was even less food around the house, because my mother gave up on cooking or grocery shopping altogether and meals became deli sandwiches at *Charlies Aunt* in Chatham and lunches with her business associates at *The Fifty Yard Line* in Chatham Township. There, I savored black bean soup flavored with *winter savory* served with tiny bowls of chopped hard-boiled egg, chopped white onion, minced parsley and wedges of lemon. The refrigerator held nothing but dried up crusts of deli sandwiches.

## Working

I took a series of jobs beginning at age 14 and was no longer able to babysit for the Wittes. My first job was at the Pizzaria e Ristorante next to Llewellen Farms in Chatham Township. The place is still there, now *Zio Gino Pizzeria e Grill.* The original owners were an extended family fresh off the boat from Corsica. I was their only employee and the only person there who spoke English.

I was hired as a server in the small dining room to help the sister, a pleasant woman in her late twenties to mid-thirties, with a tall, black, lacquered beehive hairdo, but frequently I was called up front to settle disputes at the carryout pizza counter. Given the language difficulties, orders were often mixed up. The call, *"Window! Window!"* would be announced and I would rush up front, relieved to set down my tray, as I was a terrible waitress. I would then try my best to negotiate solutions to misplaced anchovies. Sometimes the arguments had gotten quite heated by the time I arrived. I was called *Window* the entire nine months that I worked there. There was no need to correct them. The grandparents of the family made me small loaves of crusty bread from pizza dough and stood over me insisting they watch as I eat the warm bread, slathered with melting, (real) butter. At Christmas they spent days preparing a special dish for the family, which they invited me to eat with them. A few days after our feast they carried in a hefty encyclopedia and pointed to the picture of what we had eaten. It was squid. In the red sauce it had tasted like crunchy chicken.

After another job that my mother arranged for me at a gift shop in Chatham that sold Royal Doulton figurines, I made the decision to return to high school. This was after its owner made inappropriate comments about my "child-bearing hips" as he stood over me while I squatted to dust the lower glass display shelves. My grandmother agreed to pay the tuition to The Gill School. There I made pottery and occasionally attended other classes with the cute, dethroned Estonian royalty brother and sister and the Johnston & Johnston brothers of no-more-tears shampoo fame. Slipping around the trees on the former Bernardsville estate I was offered marijuana, and I intercepted debutantes on LSD trips in the girl´s bathroom. There I met Ducky, a girl hell-bent on trouble, whose father was the CFO of Red Devil caulk company. It was Ducky´s idea to run away and go to the California commune a teacher had told us about. She enlisted her older, red-neck boyfriend to take us to the highway in his pickup truck, from which we threw out our textbooks with glee.

Her father flew down twice in the company plane to fly us back to northern New Jersey. Once we were locked up in a cell in a women`s prison as we waited for him. In the shower we were surrounded by the inmates. To make conversation with a somber, dark skinned young woman standing very close to me and holding the bar of soap, I asked what she was in for. "I killed my husband", she said pensively. The inmates were not at all amused by the rich girls in prison for hitchhiking on an interstate highway and our climbing on the cell bars really ticked them off. The second time her father flew down we had been turned in by the driver of the *driveaway car* that Ducky had found on a Drew bulletin board, who had accepted our payments of 40 dollars each toward gas to get to California. My mother sent a Western Union telegram to the police giving me an *Emancipated Minor* status, so I was left behind. I made it to the commune down a long, dusty road behind a Brussel sprout farm in Davenport, near Santa Cruz after travelling with a young policeman and his wife and toddler in a school bus that broke down, stranding us for a week in Lovelady, Nevada as we awaited the repair part. I returned not much worse for wear to graduate with my class at Madison High School. I have no idea what happened to Ducky. The public high school preppy girls wanted to know about my adventures, but I stayed to myself. Thanks to Mr. Koch, a wonderful guidance counselor, I was accepted at Missouri Valley College. The school was in a place so nondescript that its biggest claim to fame was that it was only 30 miles from Sedalia, Missouri, where the turn of the century ragtime piano genius Scott Joplin had composed the Maple Leaf Rag.

After two semesters I moved to the university town of Columbia, Missouri. Here I found true egalitarianism. Everyone seemed to have the same wealth and status. I found the *wholesomeness* I craved. I married my Columbia-born husband at a potluck wedding at Stephens College, where I eventually graduated with a journalism degree. After one year in Hutchinson, Kansas as the Promotion Director for KHCC-FM, (where my unfiltered loathing of the station manager for his filthy jokes and unwanted neck rubs limited my tenure), I returned to Columbia. Columbia was my home for fifteen years. I became a community leader here, leading the food coop, being a radio personality, starting a vegetarian restaurant. I wrote poems that no one saw. They were mostly silly nonsense poems. Here are two I recall from memory:


### *Halloweenie*
*October, 1976*


The wicked wind was gone by noon,
the trees a ceased their moan.
Silence came to the red dog lame and the corn
shocks rocked no more.
The Witches Hour comes soon.

Black, shiny iridescent crows sweep over the
full cream moon´ they flutter and caw,
they scrape on the ground
and skitter and flit on the grass.
The Witches Hour comes soon.

A boat shaped vessel, night is combing the sea,
casting and pulling in
the pure and scaly flesh alike.
Black, blacker are the Evil.
Melancholia are named the sweet.
The Witches Hour is here.

Not an hour or a day, but a lingering stay
she sweeps over dreams
with a black iron rake, gouging
and sowing seeds of dreary illusion
and a thousand nights´ sleep
promised poison and deep.
The Witches Hour has come again.


## Tale of Three Cats
*November 1977*

Teddy Maroon, Teddy Maroon
had a balloon to go to the moon.

Said Mimi La Chat to Teddy Maroon,
*When are you making this trip and how soon?*

Said Teddy Maroon to Mimi La Chat,
*I´m going as soon as my cold air gets hot.*
*I´m going tomorrow, I´m going today,*
*I´m going tonight, if I might if I may.*

Just then came a cat with a terrible grin,
It was Frederico, the Magnificent.
Said Fred to Ted-eye, as Mimi stood by,
*Say friend, may I go along for the ride?*

Mimi looked cross-eyed at Ted, then at Fred,
*´Tis Mi- MI who is going,*
*when all´s done and said!*

Teddy said nothing, so you needn´t ask it,
It was Mimi La Chat
who jumped in the basket.

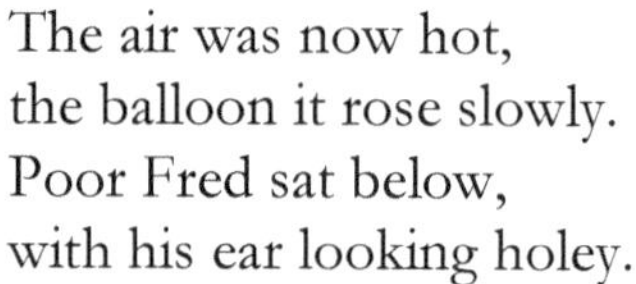

The air was now hot,
the balloon it rose slowly.
Poor Fred sat below,
with his ear looking holey.

I had to live in the Midwest before I could know that a *corn shock* existed.

# POEMS

19

*My roommate enjoying some sun, Glebe, Australia.*

# Priceless

Days I wandered the campus of Drew

University and its woods.

Nights I endured yelling and hid from the belt.

Always I scrabbled for something to eat.

In the kitchen its long, rubber counter and

massive, Chambers stove

should have stood for *hearth*.


My grandfather built this *stockbroker Tudor*.

Beyond the high-backed sink I looked

over rotten, split-rail fence across

a wooded field to where seminarians

wandered in invisible thought.


I thought I might find more

than the shrivelled apples,

the antique Junket tablets in a wooden tube

for which one needed milk.


There were ancient tins of quail eggs

with lightly rusted tops. There were slightly

chipped Meissen plates. There were endless

inedible objects of little curiosity

my mother brought home

from estate sales she worked.

Always it was the least valuable
things that we kept. Priceless things
entered and left our house quickly.
Donatello´s *bas relief* of a boy ate
cereal with me for a week. Like him, I waited
a ghost in a thin nightgown doing nothing
until asked to fold newspapers for a customer
or to move a chest of drawers.


We survived in the margins of things
bought cheaply and sold for more.
People I distrusted. They came twisted,
reeking of ill health, at all hours lying
through smiles, leaving children at home,
burning through birth rights and tuitions
to feed their addictions to things.

We asked for *Verona butter* tasted once

on a rare social visit to Frank

and Mrs Rowe´s cozy house in Verona

returning to an empty fridge with

its useless brick of colored lard.


I was led to believe

 that the presence of onions

in the house meant my mother

was a bonafide gourmet. We were told

that once, before we came along,

she had a life.

*Storm sky, Royal Botanic Gardens, Sydney, Australia.*

# Bedouin

When I go I will be a Bedouin blown

by the wind toward water, swaddled

in textiles to shield me from

stinging sands.


I´ll carry only the clothes on my back

and rugs that establish territory

for days´ rest and nights´ rest

and pillows and towels and blankets

and art that remind me who I am.


What I wear will not be important

What I look for will be.

Always I will be looking ahead

for the green and glistening tree.

# My Mulatto Onion

*February 2018*

On the second slicing

I noticed her aureole,

red blurring translucent white lines,

Not red, not entirely white.


The skin of copper slipped

Off a purple shoulder.

Unflinching on the bleached cutting board,

Lavender smiled up at the knife.


Not bitter, and not sweet,

crisp, by God, as God meant crisp!

Lifts mankind's avocado, beans and cheese,

a tomato collaborator!


This lovely human mess.

This burrito is complete.

This smallest world we know, the palate´s

delicious disobedience.

# Occasion
*April 8, 2011*

I do very well with other's rejects
and this is all you need to know about me:
The reject rack at TJ Maxx -
angora sweaters made by Twiggy.
Every house I've ever owned –
rejected first by a client.

The smart muscle cars bought for hundreds
and sold a decade later for the same cost
with only a set of tires and a
couple of batteries in between.

My pound puppy curled near my reject cat
found at closing time on a Friday,
smuggled in a borrowed carry-on
to a Key West airplane.

Always there is an occasion.
Always there is one more
to rescue in this world of strays.

# Where I'm Going with This Poem

When you open your mouth
Birds come out flying
To the sky.

When you open your mouth
The sun comes out shining
from behind grey clouds.

No one speaks of such things:
Heaven on Earth.
Your tongue is like velvet.
Your voice is a kiss.

*Jubilee Park, Glebe, Australia.*

# In the Sweat Lodge
*January 1 2009, 2019*

We made ourselves a sauna
from scavenged scraps.


We borrowed salvaged tarps
and stinky sleeping bags.


We curved and buried saplings
in the ground to make a dome.


We wrapped the covers around
the dome to pad it from the cold.


We gathered fallen tree limbs
to burn to heat the rocks.


We dug a pit. We carried in
shovels full of singeing rocks.


We crawled in, settling
hip to hip and chest to knee.


Someone would pat a stray foot
back from nearing the hot rocks.

A chant began to a monkey god, *Shree Rama,*
*Rama, Rama, Bunga ranghi Hanuman,*

*Bunga ranghi Hanuman, Bunga ranghi*
*Hanuman, Bunga ranghi Hanuman – Mahari.*

We sang roses filling hollows in the dark.
When we were hot, we went outside.

We covered our shoulders only, knowing
in our nakedness we all looked alike.

We worked part time as nurse aids.
Two days´ work paid our monthly rent.

Weapons were sent to war lords.
US death squads murdered Catholic nuns.

We hosted speakers fed in bungalows
at potlucks based on rice and beans.

We hosted Noam Chomsky, Wendell
Berry and Holly Near.

We organized for safe energy.
We organized for peace.

When *Welfare for the Wealthy*
was poured like treacle down throats,

we made ourselves a grocery store.
We made ourselves a radio station.

They blamed the red and black and brown.
They blamed the women and the queers.

They came for Aaron Schwartz,
Seth Rich, Chelsea Manning and Red Fawn.

They came for Vanessa Dunden,
Julian Assange and Muhiyidin D'baha.

They came for the white farmers´ lands.
They made the truth illegal.

In Missouri´s cold seasons we bent
like saplings to the weekend´s sweat lodge.

In our nakedness we all looked alike.
In our nakedness, they fear us.

*My home is in the middle of an untamed copse.*

# Here lies Ginger, full of Grace
## *2010*

I wanted you to know I buried Ginger, my dog, Thursday, September 23, 2010. Wednesday night she ran off and came back delighted at finding something disgusting to roll in. Then she hopped into the car and visited our old house with me, running up three flights of stairs. On Thursday morning I found she had vomited eight places in the house. I took her for a short neighborhood walk, which she wanted to do but did only with great effort. I carried her partly back. In the car she rode with the window open, smiling into the wind. For the first time ever she did not argue with being at the vet's and she sat on the chair. They rushed her in. Elderly Dr. Patrick took me to his small room and showed me the x-ray of her massive spleen tumor. Ginny knew it was time to go. Her lovely brown eyes looked at mine without fear and with trust. I called Katherine in New York before the killing shot of anesthesia. As we waited for the sedation to kick in I lay on the floor with Ginger and let her lick my mouth and the tears from my eyes. I lifted her to the table and Dr. P administered the larger dose of anesthesia and she slipped peacefully away. He carried her out the back door, allowing me to cry freely. I didn't wail but did babble, trying to make sense of death and how the lives go on. When I got home, I asked a neighbor, Nita, to stay with me until my friend arrived to help me bury Ginger. The neighbor's daughter Sarah and I started clearing the site under an ancient, white camellia tree next to Dinky, the cat I buried this spring. I am so grateful for Katherine's wonderful watercolor of Dinky and Ginny at our house in Fiddlers Marsh! Soon, Suzy arrived with a shovel followed by our mutual friend, Elizabeth. The four of us were fairly helpless against the roots and bricks that mysteriously seem to cover the yard just a few inches under the soil so Suzy called her burly friend, Neil. He relieved us to go inside and make daiquiris. Phil, an elderly house guest who had found me through the Unitarian church accommodations book arrived during this time. He managed to say that he had packed two limes "for some reason," which happened to be daiquiris. 12-year old Abbie from a few doors down was another of Ginger's friends. She brought over her dad's post hole digger and his promise to help after their soccer game. The hole was dug and Suzy and Elizabeth helped me lower Ginger into the very deep hole and cover her. She was so beautiful, and so at peace.

Sitting on the porch with Suzy eating homemade black bean nachos she said what I had fleetingly thought, but could not put into words: Ginger's passing freed me, opening wider doors to new adventures. While we visited I received a call with a full price offer on our old house, the one Ginger had shown to the prospective buyers with me the night before.

Grace is the word that described Thursday and the days since. Ginger was a dog full of Grace, in death as in her joyful, loving and inquisitive life. Everyone who knew her was touched by her. I would like to try and live more like Ginger, enjoying each day and accepting its limitations - especially celebrating the limitations. I am so moved by friends and neighbors and family to remember what it is like to have a life worth living. Thank you for sharing this with me.

*Ginny on Sullivans Island, South Carolina.*

# One Day

One day
Wonder.
People smiling,
lame,
but smiling.

One day
Nothing.
Broken computer, broken
dreams, all alone.

One night
Dreams of sunlight.
One night
Dreamless, peaceless abyss.

This is my life. This
is your life. This is our life
tied by days and nights.
This is our lives tied by suffering.

# The Last Apples Bought
### *Early August 2009*

The last apple pie

the last load of laundry

I fold your clothes neatly

and stack them in an order on your bed.

The sport socks nest belonging

to each other in this rough world

But you no longer belong to me,

but to this rough world.


Your world is full of juice -

The Big Apple!

You gorge on Mamoud's falafels

Sashay down Union Square

Are dancing in weeks with

Sufjan Stevens on stage

on free passes from Tisch

friends working lighting.


You lie on floors of aged, tiger oak

at Yoga to the People.

Your life is sepia, lit in brownstones

I only know from photos.

I´m left beached in Carolina

like a hermit crab

with no use for this shell -

a museum no one visits.


37

But finally, at least I get to buy the pears

I love, which would not keep

with apples you demanded

and I could not eat

because they always gave me gas.

*Restoration project by the author, Charleston, South Carolina.*

# Going to Tel Aviv
### *Christmas 2010*

I am not going to Tel Aviv.
It's the baby who goes,
her round cheeks still rising
like mounds of dough.

The airport table between us
is brown and button-sized
but it could be an ocean.
Silence roils off the tarmac
and through this thick glass window.

Helplessly, I tell her that her eyes
are the color of the green tea
she cradles in a bold, new way
with hands that once were traced
on brown paper making me
Thanksgiving turkeys,
flightless birds, like me.

Coatless, in pin feathers
she heads toward the snow.
*18 inches* I say. She says she knows.
But, her eyes are dancing

a laser show at my black screen.
I see her as a drop of milk
in a stroboscopic photo of a pail
of milk, in which the aureole
is a ring of phallic missiles -
Syrian, Iranian, Palestinian aimed
at sidewalks of shimmering blond girls.

At the rubber conveyor belt -
always moving away - we hug and hug
and hug as many times as I want.
We say *I love you* and I kiss
as if my lips were magnets
that could hold onto her cheeks.

But, my hand propels her forward
in her new, steel-toed boots.
The last thing I see is her wings
poking through
the thin beige sweater,
a cast-off of mine.

# Grocery Store
*Spring 2011*

Every day deserves its own tools.

This day I was her life raft,

the woman with the cat

and the semi-famous husband

so that she was always alone.

Her lime green t-shirt

embellished with pink poesies was

so young only her recent grandchild

should wear it in public.


On another day, it is her breath

mustering the wind to blow me west.

She calls my silhouette *dazzling*

against this sunrise,

*and a new one*

*just as good every day.*

But today she chatters -

there is no kinder way to say it -

about brownie mixes, her brand not carried
her travails to two, no three
stores, waiting for the manager,
*out of stock here, special order there*
working my cervical vertebrae hinge
like a nodder bisque made in Occupied Japan.
Through my clenched smiles
all I can think of
is the gasoline wasted, and why?
Why buy a mix?

# Women are the Water

*April 4, 2011*

I am not the sandy island you swim to.
I am the water surrounding living cells.
I´m the liquid on which
your thoughts bob or sink.

White Ibis wings
may land for a cool drink.
They may feather your hair like
the fingers of a woman´s hand.
They drink my water.

You've spent a lifetime looking
for island paradises to control,
believing that when you spit
you are watering a garden.
Spit´s my water, too.

I am the water surrounding living cells
and I swallow tears shed
and unshed, until a river
engulfs you with its irresistible force.

I am warm trickle of milk,

swelling of the field corn,

the sweat on your brow.

I lull boulders into becoming sand.


You without water are nothing.

Bloodless, dry bone without muscle.


Wind carries voices singing.

The women are carrying fishes on their heads.

They move like giraffes move,

necks and limbs in beautiful syncopation.


You lift up your head to cry out.

Not a sound is heard. Not

a sound is heard. Not a sound is heard.

Your mouth is dry.

# My Mount Pleasant Porch

My home is in the middle
of an un-tamed copse, dark with curling
live oak, hickory and fern.

Underbrush arches over Hobcaw Creek's
flashing Cyclopean eye
like brow on bone holding in silver fish
flowing by foundation block piers
of Remley`s Point *freedman's* shanties.

A galleon ballast stone hurled across
the Cooper River would hit first the industry
in the Neck, spook then the Citadel, mark the
Medical University, pock the College and
wreak havoc on the roses planted
in fill at White Point Gardens.

By the fifties, walking dirt roads here
toward segregated schools,
white-eyed children waved shyly at
men on dark boats going somewhere.
Negatives, familiar, like them.

The roads got a frosting of licorice asphalt.
Creosote pilings burrowed in pluff
mud cake like birthday candles.
The smell of salt and grease and little,
rotting lives turning mineral is a smell
that cannot be washed off with soap.
This is why prayer is needed.

See the trees felled by men sweating
in the three-season heat?
Smell the rubber tires burning as they
groan over stubbled ground
building the new *Durst Hospital*?

Hear the brick trucks rumbling down
South I-26 from North Carolina?
See the Orangeburg sewer pipes
lurid orange in the mud?

The Indians, the *Wando* and *Etiwan* left
words so beautiful for this land and water
they must have meant the world itself;
feel them in your mouth –
*Wappetaw, Hobcaw, Abcaw.*

Cruel street signs appeared,
repainted each year in Charleston Green

marking slavery as marketable *chic;*
*Creole Plantation,* and *Overseers Retreat.*


I tasted wild, waxy persimmons as often as
I could, before the vacant lot on the marsh
was sold.  I heard the quail squabbling in pens
kept by old Mayor Coleman behind
the Greenwich Street graveyard.


I startled a last wild turkey
last week in the small wood behind my house.
Listen, history is unreliable.
Let´s just listen to today.
The sounds are gurgling water and
rushing overhead, shushing leaves like
taffeta, squirrels walking like saints on water.


Green tree frogs shrill nonstop, unseen.
Toads plop in the pond whenever I come near.
Bull frogs thrum. The red-headed woodpecker
knocks w*hoa-whoa-whoa-whoa-whoa*
on rotten hickory trunk
announcing my time for tea.


Magnolias sputter pods to the ground.
Termites burrow. Moles tunnel.
Acorns press purely into bare feet soles

and knock to the ground anyone
foolish enough to be wearing shoes.

Roots trip us. Greenhouse pansies go
flying over furious, tiny shoulders heaving
to bury nuts in my softened beds.
I rip out seedling roots one by one in
a month in our seasonal dance.

Here in this holiest of places, all of
the greens are backlit like stained glass.
Understory and overstory,
this is a cathedral
that explodes my heart forever.

# Zeus

*July 3, 2011*


*You will never know*

*how much this means to me*


We step back to see a large dog,

a *labradoodle*, more like a sheep

lanky, and seventy pounds.

You could not quite see his eyes,

but somehow knew they were round

and brown and moist with a *joy de vivre*.

His spirit reached at least

three houses down from his home

with the little girl, plump and bright as a robin,

near the path through the trees to the playground

where he chased the sun and marveled, Sphinx-like

at the whiteness of the moon.


Three owners had thrown him away

before he found this home

with two handicapped women.

His exuberance could snap a person's bones.

His muddy clodhoppers tore off coat breast buttons.

His colossal forehead crashed against bone

for cerebral meetings of the minds.

*You have no idea what he's done*

*to the inside of our house,*
said the girl to the neighbor
with the Dutch-cut Standard Poodle.

With the father who wore a heavy gold
neck chain, with the two women and one girl,
Zeus buckled down, found himself, his
calling as a therapy dog!
Brought home gold trophies, one after
another, sending
the Lhasa Apso yapping,
frenzied with envy.

So, after the car trip
with his Lhaso riding 600 miles
to see his girl at summer camp,
he lay down his big, hard head
on the soft woman's breast and
succumbed to kidney failure.
He was found like broken glass
and smoothed with a sea of patience.
His job was well done.

May we all one day step
forward into the light of Zeus.

for Abbie, Kristi and James

# Bicycle Ride

In the mornings I've noticed
smells are sharper.
The trash is not yet set out.
Nothing is ripened by the sun.
The air is fresh, untarnished
by exhaust fumes.

A thin, polished mahogany man
with fuzzy, Malcom goatee
bicycles by, his white t-shirt just
pulled from plastic, I see. Passing, he
nods, perfuming the air
with a trail of *Cashmere Bouquet.*
I ride a half a block in his blessing.

Orange Monarch butterflies fizz
over garish, yellow lantana out
front of the Comfort Inn Motel.
The powdery pollen
flutters up my nose.

On the pier a morning fisherman
in pressed khaki slacks casts
his hook in flaccid water. His cologne
is heavy with sandalwood and musk.
He´s hoping to pull a wild fish
thrashing, its blood and guts
still satisfying on his hands.

Before the dew is stolen,
when the world is round again,
the cyclers trace its image
with looping foot-to-pedal.
 Before the march of atrocities begins,
it´s good to see a butterfly´s wings.
It´s good to wish for one full day of peace.

# At 11:15 pm in Harris Teeter on East Bay Street

*August 1, 2010*

Outside it was inky black and still

so hot the no see ums greased to

my elbow crease.


Inside, in Clemson Orange *Soffe* shorts,

desultory coeds clutched six packs of

respectable ale, lunch meat and cookies

and loitered near the self-checkout line.


Overhead lights snapped off aisle by aisle

urging us to move along, but no one

had anywhere urgent to go

at this hour.


The deli counter was closed up tight;

stone grey trays and frosty windows only

where buttery cheeses and rosy, pink

meats were supposed to be.


I paced at the packaged meats display

case, settling on *Buy One, Get One Free*

natural, uncured salami.

I carried both to the register

to negotiate a *buy one, pay for one-half* barter

when I saw her, the last cashier standing.


She was propped

against a podium,

her back to the parking lot.

Her face was as shiny as a melted Hershey bar.


Her blue windbreaker was pulled close

against the odds of air conditioning beating

ice darts on her head, while humidity

swamped her in heat each time the


electric doors hummed, sliding in

more customers.

Her eyes were wild in disbelief.


Fifteen years before she might have walked

to work, preferred to buy her own

food at the Vegetable Bin. That was before

the city's *liberal* mayor *liberated* the poor,


bulldozed public housing to sweep up river views

for private housing that he sold along

with a stadium bearing his name.

Now she travels 90 minutes for work
that pays no more now than it did then.
She transfers to three buses,
walking between the stops.

Where there are no benches or shelters,
or she pays three hours´ wage
for a ride in a smelly, littered taxi.

My uncured salami could cure nothing.
I couldn't ask her
to do another thing, except to go home
to her kids and sleep well.

In the lot I passed the policemen,
both salamis pressed under my arm,
hoping he´d think I was stealing.
It didn't come up. He looked tired, too.

# Emblem of Wishful Thinking

The one who has a tattoo on his neck

To ward on many kisses from women -

Long-limbed, full-bosomed

and smelling impossibly of peaches

is scarred for life, regardless.

*Luster Laundromat, Glebe Point Road, Glebe, Australia.*

# This Dress
July 2001

This dress I wear is invisible,

sometimes nothing more than a lotion

between showers.


This dress I wear for you is open throated

cut to the naval, slit up to there.

For this treacherous journey to you

I choose Manolo Blahnik stilettos

knowing that your one finger can throw me.


This dress is cerise; *cherries*, in French

clinging, flouncing crepe.

Cuts a path through the post office

through the sidewalks, through dull meetings,

everywhere I go.


This dress is light as silk, thick as wool.

This dress is warm as angora, cool as water.

This dress I wear is transparent.

I feel naked in public when I wear it.

This dress draws attention –
Women asked where I purchased it
Men want to sniff it, to rub it on themselves.

This dress is smoky blue,
so transparent I swear it
is made of your skin, sloughed off
without a thought
from your thighs pedaling foreign hills,
from your back tossing in a strange bed
and sent down the drain with
another woman´s shampoo.

Do you know, this dress has become
my favorite and I take it off
to launder only with reluctance?
That I am frightened beyond reason each time
that it will come back shrunken,
drained of color, or not – lost altogether?

This is a dress I frankly lived without for years.
Now I wonder how to get more years from it,
impossibly more years than fabric usually delivers.
I want to create memories in this dress.
I want this dress to figure into small histories.

But, here it is another long night

and, I have to take down the dress

and sleep in it.

I know it will become horribly creased,

or I will rip it from misuse.

But, how do I know how to handle this dress?

It worries me because,

there is not another dress in the world

that fits and flatters so well,

and I feel I must have this dress.

# How to Figure Out if the New Guy is a Man, or Some Weird Hybrid
### *Spring 2011*

1. If he whines about:

    a)  his work or other "dilemma"

    b)  about "not really knowing anyone here"

    c)  his bad breakup

    d)  his aging body or his bald spot

    e)  being cold

2. If he acts strangely innocent for his age about common social customs or conventions

3. If he doesn't give you his work number and/or email address.

4. If he calls and texts many times a day and his persistence doesn't really make sense because you have nothing really to talk about.

5.  If you even suggest he's just on a booty call and he gets offended or defensive

6.  If he ever even THINKS about having sex without a condom

7.  If you say you don't want to have sex and he tries to anyway

8.  If he is too old not to have children, or has children he rarely sees

9.  If he is inordinately proud of his feet or some other body part in the way a normal person would only feel about their recently born child's feet or other body part

10. If he has a weird, girlish child's type of nose

11. If you find him an uninteresting person but feel you have to spend time with him to be nice

12. Remember, a lot of things have a penis and still, they are not men

# Missteps
### *May 8, 2011 (Mother's Day)*

The tattooed guy – Let´s call him Chad

could have been on this pew two years

since before I could look at him

straight-on, as you wouldn't

a midget, or an obesely fat person.


It's a tossup,

which was his most effective choice

in signifying terror – mine, or his -

the eyebrow markings like Frankenstein

- stitches for all I know, that may

have a name borrowed from embroidery,


or the nose, pierced and stretched

- where septum normally holds nostrils apart -

- to a low hole, gouging

unwanted images of pounded

orifices valued at nothing but betrayal.


Something has largely shielded me

from todays' price for his mistakes.

My own scarifications are as willful

to be sure, but my pain is well-hidden.

I bury my screams in sunscreen.

He attends Sunday school more than I do.
One time when my number was in
the church bulletin, he called me, urgently
soliciting a ride to my house for a meeting,
not realizing I would be too busy cooking
and cleaning to leave, so I told him
and left him wherever he was.

Yesterday, I made the mistake of trusting
a possible customer. I drove him
around three towns swallowing insults and the lie
he had intention to buy any houses from me,
as he was learning my business, and I
was nothing; someone he stiffed.

My neighbor, whose husband can explain
the Confederate flag on his bumper as
a symbol of American freedom and
independent thought, brought
me pound cake today
to celebrate her new oven.

I lift a collapsed eggplant onto a cool plate.

Season its blandness with salt and cumin.

I make this baba ganouj with

rancid sesame butter, pouring away

the oil, hoping to reduce

the worst of its toxins.


Too broken to mix things just right,

my biggest mistake is accepting

the sins of others as my own.

Until now. Those who are not quite right

yet, are quite rightly present, the

shaman, the confessional ones,


The ones turned inside out for all to see

in spite of themselves,

without any real choice in the matter,

show us 24/7 the shape

of the human soul.

Dancing on, ever awkwardly, dancing on.

*True American Tradition, Glebe, Australia.*

# Governors Cup Fishing with Paula
### *July 12, 2001*

Underneath the smiling, lemon peel moon,

undulating in between vast and inky satin sheets

underneath the loneliness, the laziness, the shame

under mast and boom and crane,


On the decks of *Siked Out, Play Deep,*

*Laid Back, Skee Bo,*

*Risky Business* - other names for boats you know,

underneath the scent of perfume,

smoky cigarettes, salty tang of tuna,

Sighting the filet knife men slice open

bellies oozing bloody entrails;

fresh pompano and wahoo.


Young girls flutter in 12" skirts

butterfly kisses abound around

Sunburnt men so happy, up at 4 am

at 6 pm hosing down million-dollar bows

to show us stepping aboard their winnings.


Passing sashimi, Ritz crackers,

boat-made yellowfin tuna-shrimp dip

*Made with 140 ingredients*

says a most brilliant chef of the South,
jubilant, a building framer by trade.
Undulating on the waves
precariously like toddlers
boy-men sleep like babies
curled in tiny berths,

their fists still tightly balling poles.
Dreaming wads of sweaty cash and
the engraved Rolex watch promised
by the boat owner, *Bring it on,*
says Walker.

In the nest of Ray Bans, charts,
Halloween-sized bags of Snickers
beer cans, sharp things, hooks
and pillows, the undulating sway
of a woman´s hips rocks them
all to sleep each night.

We go no further than Charleston
Harbor Resort & Marina, yet this is
a white city of boats, 102,
The biggest winners in *Catch and Release*
of all the marinas entered this year.
The crew and captains´ names are unknown
but the world is in their bloodshot eyes.

# Southern Man's Zen
*2001*

67

You really can´t quite

see through the polite

A Southern man´s mama taught him.


He´ll craft a certain joy

to entertain - the boy.

Not to disappoint is what brought him.

# Shade
## *2011*

Things hold memories.
This is well known, of course.

So, in the curve of the silk
lampshade I see
the side of the road lamp shop
with Katherine on that trip to
St. Augustine when she was eleven.
My forced joviality, my sadness & my grief
were permanently stiffened open like
the wired taffeta.

Maybe things can set us free.
Repositories of our foolishness.

Bearing witness to our dreams
for a perfect living room,
for a perfect childhood,
they don´t laugh out loud. They don´t
venture an opinion. They know it doesn't matter.
You did the best you could. Yes, you failed and
yes, you overpaid, and still you´re not in fashion.

The lampshade was outdated
when you bought it.

But is a life well-lived
ever really *fashionable*?
and, whatever it costs, shouldn´t we get
as much enjoyment from it as possible?
And, at the end of the day aren´t you
stalwart enough to get the job done?

You shield the harshest glare
from the bulbs, at the end of the day.

*Author and unnamed camel, Birubi Bay, Australia.*

# Many Worlds, One Sun
*October 10, 2009*

I have always winced when introduced

to a *Lakesha* or a *Shameka,*

with the word blazing like a jailhouse tattoo

in a prominent place.

Like, what parent gives

the child the nails and hammer

to her own coffin at birth?


Why give your child an outsider´s name

when it´s such a little thing to give wings?

With a *Mark* or a *Susan* she could sail over

troubles on soft currents, airborne.


I watched a slow-paced movie, *Goodbye, Solo.*

A Senegalese cab driver whose

real name was *Soulemane,* who

made a commitment, stalks

a stranger to prevent the stranger´s suicide.


By sensible Western standards, this man

was without motivation, Christlike

and the stranger didn´t like it or him one bit,

but, the fictional immigrant who made his life

from the bits of another´s unearthed my life,

Shook the dirt of fear of death alone
of fear of already being dead in a way,
right from my roots,
replanting me somewhere unknown.

And, I was struck with the realization
that those *black parents and brown parents,*
as Cornell West distinguishes, for another
reason I do not know, those parents
glibly applying the hot needle
and the ink to a defenseless newborn, are
in the act of trying to create a
whole, new world I might want to visit.

And I realize my anger is not
for their children at all, but, here
we go again - it´s all about me -
for myself because I need them.
I need their dark-skinned and strange
children in my world. Their pungent
skin smelling of old wood and curry,
their unfathomable devotion to hair styles,
because like I always say, I need choices.

The truth is I cannot share

the world with the word *no*

and resent all gates that are closed.

Without wonder and mysteries to try

and inhabit, or like lions, to know

they still exist in some places, I feel like

I am inhabiting no place at all.

*Katherine and Sherrietta, kindergarten graduation, Charleston, South Carolina.*

# Knot

*January 2009*

The thrill of wood
the satin sheen of it
A kind of skin, but without
all that tiresome emotion

Leaning into a 140-year old demi-lune
column of 2,000-year old oak tree
at Circular Congregational Church,
I want to become like the wood,

the way it smells like a human
was once alive, gave birth to other trees
needed dirt, air, and water
to live - not much -
gave shade to creatures small and large

like fragrant lilac, pungent persimmon
food – acorns, apples, peaches for pie
pine nuts, pollen for honey bees
maple syrup for children`s delight

tree homes/homes in the trees

Indigo buntings/red birds with black wings

white-chested osprey/white

squirrels from Megget

Listening like live oak for 300 years

in parks they cannot leave

drinking in confessions of mothers

failed businessmen, dances of newlyweds.

happiness, sorrows.

Upholding the weight of this congregation

holding the pavers on Chalmers Street

holding the slaves in the holds of the slave ships

holding my potluck salads, camping stews

holding dinner in front of televisions.

Giving still; knife handles, chopping blocks

French oak for garnet Beaujolais

a barrel/a bed/a house/ a shed

wood for the shed

heat/ potash/potassium/ash

Heated black to spread like silk as

war paint for play Indians, for football braves

for temptresses´ kohl eyes, the *Cleopatra, Sappho,*

*Theda Baras and Kate Mosses*

Blackening fingers of artists
sketching trees on bleached sheets of trees
Bedding corn-fed beef, salmon steaks,
bedding roasting ears in cribs
bagging groceries in paper the color
of human skin.

A favorite age of wood is the middle -
calm, inert, stalwart and trusty,
the domesticated wood of the table
the bed, the pew, the stair tread.
Wood under my touch, smoothed
by drumming fingers, by decisive, flat
palms, by tear-stained cheeks
Kissed by tears, by babies´ drool,
beloved the way people burrow
into each other, leaving tiny tunnels.

Trees contour the light, temper the heat,
sweat drops of sweet water,
Suffer artillery fire, suck in
hurricane waters, exhaling all the while
so unworthy we may breathe.

Our shadows, our better selves.
Listen, as they whisper in the wind

pitying our human sins.

Shaking their heads at our willful pettiness

at our short and futile lives –

*You can't make even a decent drum stick of a*

*bone*, they sigh.

*Galveston, Texas homeowner.*

*Galveston, Texas home.*

# Small Poem About Texas
*July 2007*

This is an homage

to the good-looking police man

who pulled me over going 95

in a *70-mile per hour zone,*

found perfectly reasonable my explanation

that as it was early on in the day

and I had a 13-hour drive to make

I had to cover the most ground while

my senses were most sharp.


Let me off with a warning, marveling,

*"You don't say, ten to one?"* when I told him

the ratio of women to men in South Carolina.


I´m writing while driving

in the glint of white spring sunshine

sparking off all the glass and the

mica-painted car hoods stalled

on Main Boulevard at any hour in Austin.

I´m writing while driving

in circles backing out of UT campus dead ends.

I´m writing about driving

from one $400,000 dollar four-room

shot gun bungalow to another

to marvel at backyard outsider art

in the sun with Ed and Wendy.


And, I´m writing while driving

between Austin and Houston

where I write in the margins and

on all the white faces of the

photos in the *Houston Press*.


I´m writing in South Houston

reveling in its refreshing grittiness,

eating one of the last meals served

at Otto's BBQ Hamburgers.

The cashier, who looks like a librarian,

assures me the tea

is not weak, with a

*No, that's strong, TEXAS-ice tea,*

*unsweetened.*


I´m writing stuck in traffic next to cattle

grazing next to half-built, vinyl houses

*From the One Hundred and Tens*

In Texas, home of the legal U-Turn with
signs modeled on the upturned horseshoe
In Texas, where my Lexus scraps it´s navigation
to take up crazy-quilt embroidery instead.
In Texas, home of the happy
turquoise Valero cheap gas stations.
In Texas, where black men shuffle in the
afternoon heat, dancing the *don't that beat all*
Devil of unemployment.

In Galveston, I walk
taking pictures of ruined beauty
explained as from the last hurricane.
I eat a cheap and filling Mexican breakfast
with the mayor and his son; four dollars
for beans, tortillas, eggs and potatoes.

On the trucker route, I want to stop
everywhere, at all the small stands
sometimes only a plastic tarp tied
to 4 poles with a hand lettered sign, *Cocos Frijos*
at the off-brand convenience store,
*Handistop Food Store, at the Rosie Food Store following*
in a concrete block house painted white and
at the *$1 Taqueria* stands sprouting in old buses.

I could never have written about

*Waterloo Records* or *BookPeople*,

places I liked okey.

I could never have written about Texas at a desk.

I wrote on the road and *I reckon* I was

*riding a gravy train with biscuit wheels*

lucky I never wrecked.

# Falling off the Edge of the World
### *July 5, 2011*

Going to Australia must be like being terminally ill.

People want to help. They look at you pityingly

and also angrily, fingering their unpaid bills

glaring at ungrateful children, stuck with

neighbors who send police to their door

because they park in the street and not

their driveway.


Everyone wants a piece to say *I once almost knew her*

though here for years, they rarely called. With

such little time left, it is exhausting just

deciding which moments to share is

enough to send anyone to bed with

a headache.


The decisions to be made, putting tape on the bottles

that may or may not swell under pressure. What

to pack for a journey to a place so remote its

venomous insects, its fashion are unknown

and unknowable, and what will you be

doing there?


Undressing the home for people unknown, undressing

the people you have loved every day, undressing

yourself to body surf hoping God won´t let

you drown there alone but will send you

back, reformed.

# You Can Pack A Lot into Some Days
*June 2010, for Gloria in St. Augustine.*

Sometimes at the end of the day,

you just feel happy.

At 8 o'clock in the morning, you put on your

white bathing suit

drive to the beach for a swim but

in the parking lot the phone rings,

and it's not good news as

you are blasted in a spew of tobacco juice

but must listen. Mid-stream, the battery dies

and they will never understand that

you are burning precious gas, idling

the engine, leaning parallel

to the passenger seat, never taking

your eye off the beady red eye of the charger

fed only by force, held at an elusive angle

against the dashboard socket and that

calling this person back is out of the question

because the blood rushing to your head

makes you recall your recent resolution

reading the new word in *Readers Digest*,

*Unitasker,* to be one, so you hang up.


Somehow, by 3:00 pm

you have chosen to believe in Angels -

that's Angels, not angles -

who, it makes sense must by nature

do their work invisibly

as the two real estate agents

who keep valiantly showing

your empty house are supernatural

but still, don't get a sale, and in the fall

you will go in boredom

for a bid you cannot afford to

fix the hole in your car door from where,

as you slept upstairs, fitfully at your cousin`s

some thug shoved a thick screwdriver in to

pop your lock in Newark

and though pockmarked,

this body-man here is beatific when he says

*I'll order the paint and call you*

*when it's in and touch it up* and you say,

*yes, but how much will it cost*, and he says, *Oh,*

*I'm not going to charge you to touch it up!*

As if that is how life is done on this cloud

and you think that the tattoos on his forearms

look just like 15th century Flemish

manuscript illuminations, and just

as this idea is heating up

you pull into your carport and steel

yourself for the mailbox-spider bite, tabloid

meat creations, latest Bank of Criminals hoax,

a truck swings up beside you and a
broad-shouldered brown man in a broad
straw hat hops out, laughing,
bearing pine straw, beaming when you
wonder aloud if he is also an angel,
though he insists on being called *Diablo*
and, you'll take him that way,
as you're half-Unitarian, anyway.

At 8:00 PM no one knows
you are still in your bathing suit
with friends reading poetry
behind Dock Street Theatre
walking a cobblestone street
amazed that this day of all days
you wore sensible shoes to the surprise
at the end of the rainbow;
an art gallery where miraculous cheeses
and pitchers of daiquiris await you,
and because it is summer, and it is a
bathing suit you wear, you lift
your cover- up to show the suit
which reminds you,
you have a membership to a pool downtown
where, while the water seems cold at first
you realize it's just cool,
which is exactly what you would

prefer at the end of a long and sticky day.

You don't look so bad in the mirror naked,
hanging your suit on the sauna's
temperature gauge
as you lie pleasantly
in the dark waiting for animal satiety.
The suit dries in no time to wear home.

At the desk, just because you ask,
the attendant gives you two free passes,
though they never do that
and this time the phone rings and it's a friend
who is not sanding floors tomorrow
so will help you paint in the morning
and his wife is making
another brown-eyed cherub and
you step out of the building into
a sky painted Prussian blue,
clean limbs, lightened and
all the leering stars twinkle overhead,
with all the kisses that
Angels have in store for you.

# Woman Met at the Philadelphia Airport with Family Waiting

It was on a plane from Abu Dhabi

that their fate was flung


The clot struck 23 hours after takeoff,

confined in a cabin.


Her husband lumbered to the gangplank

and sank to his knees, fish eyed.


She plated the table with

dinner for seven in Saddle River, New Jersey.


Eleven years passed. She is waiting in an airport

for a broken plane to be fixed.


*This is my Joe, this is my Martha, my Steven, my*

*Billy, my Frieda. And this is my Frank.*


A fat and happy family looks lucky

in Christmas sweaters.


A voice interrupts us announcing a bus

has been located to drive us to Newark. We nod.

She palms me another, a recent one of *Martha*,
now 17, with *Freida*; broad, Mexican shoulders in charge

while she goes to move a cranky father
into a nursing home.

*Billy* and *Steven*; half-brothers, *half-breed*
*Apaches* spat from South Texas,

*Frieda,* their surprise baby
after they'd adopted the first two.

Her phone rings. *More money for pizza.* She
whispers low, rolls her eyes at me, enjoys her time.

Waiting five hours in an airport to drive to an airport,
this silence we share bumping suitcases,

pockets weighted,
*This*, this is her vacation.

# Physics: Everything in this World

The night house speaks in squeaks,
sighs and thuds.
A rustling stirs the den.
I listen in my bed,
white-eyed for the dog's familiar tag clink.
No dog, instead a sharp one-two crack
from a specific oak floor board
a ping from the fireplace
brick and mortar, black steel on glass
hickory logs charred half to ash
a gurgle from the bathroom
somewhere under its tile over diagonal,
tongued planks, copper
pipes idle water over the earth.

There are no ghosts in this
contented, sober house,
but floating over everything
in the blackness is every color;
the symphony of everything,
every possibility in this world.

I wake up to a day pregnant
with rain, singing a Beatles song,
*A Day in the Life.*
Fried potatoes, sweet and salty.
Everything in this world.

# We're the sort you don't want
*April 19, 2013*

So, I want too much. Shoot me, Sheriff Al Canon. Shoot me, Senator Lindsay Graham, shoot me, Wayne LaPierre. Shoot me Tea Partiers, who know no joy. Grab your PAID FOR BY THE 1% right to buy guns and shoot me, and all the starry-eyed children who stand near me, because you cannot blind us to what is wrong with cheaper TVs, or salt-sugar-fat satiation on the tongue, and you'll never get us all. We're the sort you don't want.

*NSW Farmers anti-fracking rally, Sydney, Australia.*

# The Head, the Heart, and the Body
*2010*

There's a balance somewhere

between porousness and rock hardness

an emulsification of those two

so that everything is exquisite, yet bearable.

But it seems every blasted day

I have to crouch against the blows,

cradling the head

lest the brains get smashed in.


With dumb hope, they'll be used again.

Forget glimpsing the tree top lace finery.

Forget swaying, listening to joy.

Yet I can't forget, like a mental patient

who pummels his own head,

I must remember.


There´s a balance somewhere

between giving and taking

between self and other so that

it´s not hard being perfectly alone.

If it comes to that, and it may,

that edge is where I long to belong

that shelf, perched. perfectly content

on the ribbon of my own confines.

# Marvella of West Baltimore, She Says

*October 23, 2017*

What are poems?

Poems are pepper on a bland potato.

And, most people can find pepper.

It is black and it is completely different

from salt, which is white.


When I name something,

It´s only out of love.

Fearsome things I do not name.

I let them die unnamed.


I´m a person who prefers wooden objects

to people. Cherry wood seduces me

with satiny, perfumed sheets.

I´m satisfied to dance on hearts of pine.


Memories of axes, sparks

flying, horrendous roaring of saws

snug copses of children, all gone -

Let memories fly like sparks, I say!

Caeiro, the shepherd was given paper
by a papelaria on the mountain.
The Argonaut was born in him like a twin.
The *leaves of grass* whispered, a piece
with each step, until walking so many steps,
the poems crowded out his memory.

If I write a poem, it is not because I know
how to write a poem, but because not
writing the poem pushes me along
a path toward madness.
When nothing makes sense,
poetry makes sense.

Once, I nearly drowned.
My thin arms cut the ocean like blades.
A family died in the storm that same day.
My round belly bobbed us back to the shore
where, gulping hot sun air on the sand
we declared my baby a Miracle.

Later, I tried all the names that I knew,

the magical names of creatures I knew -

*Calvin, Alexander, Heidi,*

*Dorothy, Theodore, Lila, and Mignon,*

women whose names I knew,

or people I thought I knew.


Rolling on the hospital trolley

*Katherine* came to my lips like

a sudden kiss on a cupped face.


Like the sky smiling forever,

she stayed for a while and was gone.

Why does the sky suddenly change

to something unrecognizable?

Why are both the sun and the rain

in hiding at the same time?


If it rains or doesn´t rain, this is something

God must work out for himself!

I can be churlish, too.

And, let me ask God about Albinism!

Yellow-white hair and milk-blue skin?

Blind children must tell jokes to bullies

in public pools to keep from crying!

I take what I'm given
and what I do not have.
I declare the potato beautiful, and
make paella from pepper.
I find rosemary growing between
a fence and a blown newspaper,
and I add that.

Not having a garden is no problem for me.
I place the chair in the room looking out
always to the branches of a living tree
and to clouds dancing weightlessly.

Marvella is a name given
by a parent so in love with her child
that she cannot think practically of its future.
Velvet, buttered popcorn, chocolate, sunshine
gentle rains, summer storms and lightening,
are all together in this single name.

Marvella is my name.
I come to you like an orphan,
like You, perhaps,
slipping in and out of continents
between shadows of sun and rain.

If it never rains, I don't care!

I keep the umbrella you gave me, just in case

I finger its scalloped edge, just like lace.

An imaginary life is the worst life to waste.

My advice is to waste the other life instead.

*Colorful woman met at train station, NSW, Australia.*

# Yet
## *2013*

To sit surrounded by green leaves

swooning against themselves,

sighing like taffeta....


The squirrels mainly leave me alone now,

after I accidentally ran one over.

The family of comet fish splash in the fountain

and dive down to where

I´ve made them caverns of blocks.

I have a memoir in my lap

*Author with dogs, Regua, Portugal.*

from the public library down the street,

across from the grocery store with the

best sweet corn and artichokes.


Yet.

I rattle around in this house

like a garnet in a coffee can.

Ouch, ouch, ouch, ouch, ouch.

Everywhere I touch hurts.

I hit boundaries of a hard place

either too big or too small.

I can't tell which.

I mean nothing here.
I'm distilled for crony capitalists
to a walking wallet, my actual life
reduced to a consumer spending history.
I want the right to stumble blind,
to make fierce, foolish mistakes.

Somewhere, water is constantly in the pond.
Comets still are swimming whether
or not I pay the electric bill.

# Find Some Things to Love
### *2019*

I made it to the train on time
cursing, in spite of, to spite the rain.
The conductor was kind
about me sitting in the wrong place, with
passengers from Beijing and San Francisco.

The ocean is right here,
next to the ribbon windows, next to
the tracks we roll on to Lisbon.
The ocean is grey with white chuffs of
- like, eyes, flashing at lies.

A man two seats over is looking
at me nicely, resting
his eyes on my face
as if it were soft petals of a flower.
I let my face be his petal-flower.

My phone charger is found
coiled securely in my purse.
I let the relief wash over me.
Surprise!
The rain has stopped.

The trucks at the industrial zone

line up to carry paper

to all the neighborhood papelarias

people go to for photo copies, drawing paper,


batteries, school book bags, knitting magazines,

gossip papers, gum erasers, document sleeves,

Fimo clay, pastel orange highlighters.

Why not love trucks today?

*My mother, Nancy Lee Hermance in The Circle.*

*You can have perfect, or you can have done.*

*- Author*

Wendy Lee Hermance was trained in journalism at
Stephens College. She worked for the University of
Missouri and Kansas Public Radio and for various South
Carolina non-profits designing programming, publications,
and writing grants.  She has written and produced freelance
features for regional publications and for *American Public
Media*. Wendy is a self-taught conservator of old buildings,
who has been recognized by the State of Maryland and the
City of Charleston, South Carolina. After 20 years in
property management, she returned to school, entering the
experimental Project Management Leadership program at
the University of Sydney. There she wrote about disaster
management, distributed workplaces, command and
control, informal networks, coordination theory,
organizations, resilience, labor law, volunteers and social
cohesion. Almost all of these topics made devotion to
termite removal or kitchen tap selection seem dull, so she
started writing again. Her first book, *What's that Stuff? A
Natural Foods Reference Guide* (now out of print) is to be
followed by her forthcoming *Weird Foods of
Portugal*. Wendy is a member of the Poetry Society of South
Carolina and a contributor to *The Avocet*. She lives.